BITS OF BIGNESS

INSPIRATIONAL NUGGETS TO REMIND
YOU OF YOUR MAGNIFICENCE

THERESA ROSE

Theresa Rose

Visit my website at TheresaRose.com for more information or
to inquire about volume discounts.

Printed in the United States of America

First Edition: May 2013

Second Edition: February 2016

Serious Mojo Publications

P.O. Box 385037

Minneapolis, MN 55438

ISBN-13 978-0981886947

This book is dedicated to all of my amazing teachers, mentors, leaders and guides who inspired me to discover my own BIGness.

Introduction

Some of the greatest lessons come from observing those who have already done what we want to do. They have paved the way, slayed the dragons of fear, and showed us what it looks like to live to our fullest potential. Their words are a roadmap to our own success if we take the time to integrate their wisdom.

We all have dreams, hopes and desires for our future. We want to have more, do more and be more. How do we get there? One of the first steps is to surround ourselves with positive messages that are in violent support of our dreams. This little book of inspiration is designed to support you on your journey to BIGness, giving you just the nudge you need to keep moving forward.

Are you ready to grow bigger, brighter and happier than you have ever thought possible? Are you ready to let go of fear and transform into the powerful being you are meant to be? Everything you need is already within you, and these words will help you discover a life of joy, prosperity, and gratitude.

May you always remember how magnificent you truly are.

Blessings,
Theresa

"You are not meant to live a life of mediocrity! You are meant to suck every last drop of juice out of your brief time on earth."

- Theresa Rose

"There's more to life than cheek bones."

– Kate Winslet

"Well behaved women seldom make history."

- Laurel Thatcher Ulrich

"How we spend our days is, of course, how we spend our lives."

- Annie Dillard

"Another year is fast approaching. Go be that starving artist you're afraid to be. Open up that journal and get poetic finally. Volunteer. Suck it up and travel. You were not born here to work and pay taxes. You were put here to be part of a vast organism to explore and create. Stop putting it off. The world has much more to offer than what's on 15 televisions at TGI Fridays. Take pictures. Scare people. Shake up the scene. Be the change you want to see in the world."

- Jason Mraz

"This isn't a dress rehearsal, baby, so let's start living juicy!"

- Theresa Rose

"But I'm kind of comfortable with getting older because it's better than the other option, which is being dead. So I'll take getting older."

- George Clooney

"Being powerful is like being a lady. If you have to tell people you are, you aren't."

- Margaret Thatcher

"People often say that motivation doesn't last. Well, neither does bathing - that's why we recommend it daily."

- Zig Ziglar

"I get those fleeting, beautiful moments of inner peace and stillness – and then the other 23 hours and 45 minutes of the day, I'm a human trying to make it through in this world."

- Ellen DeGeneres

"Every fear bubble you run into and pop makes you bigger."

- Theresa Rose

"Always be a first-rate version of yourself, instead of a second-rate version of somebody else."

- Judy Garland

Theresa Rose

"You can have anything in this world you want, if you want it badly enough and you're willing to pay the price."

- Mary Kay Ash

"Life is an opportunity, benefit from it. Life is beauty, admire it. Life is a dream, realize it. Life is a challenge, meet it. Life is a duty, complete it. Life is a game, play it. Life is a promise, fulfill it. Life is sorrow, overcome it. Life is a song, sing it. Life is a struggle, accept it. Life is a tragedy, confront it. Life is an adventure, dare it. Life is luck, make it. Life is too precious, do not destroy it. Life is life, fight for it."

- Mother Teresa

"You just have to be yourself and go full with confidence and be courageous."

- Gabby Douglas

"Fear is the perfume of my Inner Small Girl. She covers herself in it. She reeks of it. She pushes people away because of it. It's a crusty old bottle of "Charlie" for the soul. Frankly, I'd rather wear Chanel No. 5."

- Theresa Rose

"I'm tough, I'm ambitious, and I know exactly what I want. If that makes me a bitch, okay."

- Madonna

"A woman is like a tea bag; you can't tell how strong she is until you put her in hot water."

- Eleanor Roosevelt

"It is impossible to live without failing at something, unless you live so cautiously that you might has well not have lived at all, in which case you have failed by default."

- J.K. Rowling

"If we did all the things we are capable of, we would literally astound ourselves."

- Thomas Edison

"When you are in your bigness, possibility turns into probability, probability turns into inevitability, and maybe turns into yes."

- Theresa Rose

"I do believe that the single most important thing I could ever share with you with regard to maximizing the health, harmony, and happiness in your life can be summed up in just two words: Love yourself."

- Mike Dooley

"It is not living that matters,
but living rightly."

- Socrates

"Joy will keep you moving forward. Never lose sight of it. Make it a part of your life every single day."

- Theresa Rose

"God had to create disco music so I could be born and be successful."

- Donna Summer

"Be the Bigger You. Be the You that knows your awesomeness. Be the You that doesn't give credence to petty comments from insecure people. Be the You that you are destined to be. Shine your light as brightly as you can. It is not your problem if your light hurts the eyes of those blind to their own power."

- Theresa Rose

"Trust yourself. Create the kind of self that you will be happy to live with all your life. Make the most of yourself by fanning the tiny, inner sparks of possibility into flames of achievement."

– Golda Meir

"If there's specific resistance to women making movies, I just choose to ignore that as an obstacle for two reasons: I can't change my gender, and I refuse to stop making movies."

- Kathryn Bigelow

"The greater danger for most of us lies not in setting our aim too high and falling short; but in setting our aim too low, and achieving our mark."

- Michaelangelo

"Insane people are always sure that they are fine. It is only the sane people who are willing to admit that they are crazy."

– Nora Ephron

"I think the most liberating thing
I did early on was to free myself
from any concern with my looks
as they pertained to my work."

- Meryl Streep

"Women in particular need to keep an eye on their physical and mental health, because if we're scurrying to and from appointments and errands, we don't have a lot of time to take care of ourselves. We need to do a better job of putting ourselves higher on our own 'to do' list."

- Michelle Obama

"Joy can help you have more, do more and be more than you ever thought possible."

- Theresa Rose

"Today, charting your own course isn't just more necessary than ever before. It's also much easier - and much more fun."

- Pink

"Don't let what you don't know scare you, because it can become your greatest asset. And if you do things without knowing how they have always been done, you're guaranteed to do them differently."

- Sara Blakely, Founder of Spanx

"You and I are essentially infinite choice-makers. In every moment of our existence, we are in that field of all possibilities where we have access to an infinity of choices."

- Deepak Chopra

"You can choose to think that anything is possible. You can choose to think that everything is lining up in support of your dreams. You can choose to think that you can change your reaction to any circumstance at any time. You can choose to think that this moment is the only moment you have. You can choose your capabilities. You can choose to design a life instead of accepting one by default. You can choose to see the impossible as possible. You can choose."

- Theresa Rose

TheresaRose.com

"When you have a dream, you've got to grab it and never let go."

- Carol Burnett

"Be not afraid of greatness. Some are born great, some achieve greatness, and others have greatness thrust upon them."

- William Shakespeare,

Twelfth Night

"With realization of one's own potential and self-confidence in one's ability, one can build a better world."

- His Holiness the Dalai Lama

"Our interiors dictate
our exteriors."

- Theresa Rose

"Do or do not. There is no try."

- Yoda

"The most effective way to do it is to do it."

- Amelia Earhart

"If you don't 'act as if your name were on the door' it never will be."

- Patricia Fripp

"I've learned from experience that if you work harder at it, and apply more energy and time to it, and more consistency, you get a better result. It comes from the work."

— Louis C.K.

"Our limited thinking is the single biggest obstacle we have when we embark on something new."

- Theresa Rose

"A dame that knows the ropes isn't likely to get tied up."

- Mae West

"I have learned over the years that when one's mind is made up, this diminishes fear; knowing what must be done does away with fear."

- Rosa Parks

Theresa Rose

"The willingness to accept responsibility for one's own life is the source from which self-respect springs."

- Joan Didion

"Regret is for wussies."

- Theresa Rose

"If I make a fool of myself, who cares? I'm not frightened by anyone's perception of me."

- Angelina Jolie

"You can't be that kid standing at the top of the waterslide, overthinking it. You have to go down the chute."

- Tina Fey

"Dance like you belong on Solid Gold, and you will free yourself to be more than you thought you ever could be."

- Theresa Rose

"I'm gonna live till I die."

- Frank Sinatra

"Most folks are as happy as they make up their minds to be."

- Abraham Lincoln

Bits of **Bigness**

"For every minute you are angry, you lose sixty seconds of happiness."

– Ralph Waldo Emerson

58

Theresa Rose

"Holding on to anger is like drinking poison and expecting the other person to die."

- Buddha

"I believe that every single event in life happens in an opportunity to choose love over fear."

- Oprah Winfrey

Theresa Rose

"Turn feardom into freedom by saying yes more than you say no."

- Theresa Rose

"All we have to decide is what to do with the time that is given to us."

- Gandalf in The Lord of the Rings

"How wonderful it is that nobody need wait a single moment before starting to improve the world."

- Anne Frank

"You must be the change you wish to see in the world."

- Mahatma Gandhi

"Cherish forever what makes you unique, 'cuz you're really a yawn if it goes."

- Bette Midler

"It is your role in this
Divine Play to be hardcore."

- Theresa Rose

"Follow what you are genuinely passionate about and let that guide you to your destination."

- Diane Sawyer

"Your work is going to fill a large part of your life, and the only way to be truly satisfied is to do what you believe is great work. And the only way to do great work is to love what you do. If you haven't found it yet, keep looking. Don't settle. As with all matters of the heart, you'll know when you find it. And, like any great relationship, it just gets better and better as the years roll on. So keep looking until you find it. Don't settle."

– Steve Jobs

Theresa Rose

"Thank you, thank you, thank you! I deserve this; send me more!"

- Anodea Judith

"You don't need to exercise, but you absolutely have permission to play."

- Theresa Rose

"I've missed more than 9000 shots in my career. I've lost almost 300 games. 26 times, I've been trusted to take the game winning shot and missed. I've failed over and over and over again in my life. And that is why I succeed."

- Michael Jordan

"If you do what you've always done, you'll get what you've always gotten."

- Tony Robbins

"It's just better to be yourself than to try to be some version of what you think the other person wants."

- Matt Damon

"I have a head for business and a bod for sin. Is there anything wrong with that?"

- Tess in Working Girl

Theresa Rose

"If being an egomaniac means I believe in what I do and in my art or music, then in that respect you can call me that. I believe in what I do, and I'll say it."

- John Lennon

"There are two kinds of power you have to fight. The first is the money, and that's just our system. The other is the people close around you, knowing when to accept their criticism, knowing when to say no."

- Martin Scorcese

"I like having my hair and face done, but I'm not going to lose weight because someone tells me to. I make music to be a musician, not to be on the cover of Playboy."

- Adele

"Fear is the domain of small people. "

- Theresa Rose

"The ultimate measure of a man is not where he stands in moments of comfort and convenience, but where he stands at times of challenge and controversy."

- Martin Luther King, Jr.

"It is often when night looks darkest, it is often before the fever breaks that one senses the gathering momentum for change, when one feels that resurrection of hope in the midst of despair and apathy."

- Hillary Clinton

"Things change. We learn. We practice. We grow. There is a moment for all of us when we go from 'I can't' to 'I can'."

- Theresa Rose

"A good hockey player plays where the puck is. A great hockey player plays where the puck is going to be."

- Wayne Gretzsky

"It's better to hang out with people better than you. Pick out associates whose behavior is better than yours and you'll drift in that direction."

- Warren Buffet

"There are no secrets to success. It is the result of preparation, hard work, and learning from failure."

- Colin Powell

"I always find that when I do something that I like, from my heart, then it works."

- Harvey Weinstein

"Never continue in a job you don't enjoy. If you're happy in what you're doing, you'll like yourself, you'll have inner peace. And if you have that, along with physical health, you will have had more success than you could possibly have imagined."

- Johnny Carson

"Do you know what I like about comedy? You can't laugh and be afraid at the same time —of anything. If you're laughing, I defy you to be afraid."

- Stephen Colbert

"Don't cry because it's over, smile
because it happened."

- Dr. Seuss

"One must not let oneself be overwhelmed by sadness."

- Jackie Kennedy

"When I get lonely these days, I think: So BE lonely, Liz. Learn your way around loneliness. Make a map of it. Sit with it, for once in your life. Welcome to the human experience. But never again use another person's body or emotions as a scratching post for your own unfulfilled yearnings."

– Elizabeth Gilbert

Theresa Rose

"Some changes look negative on the surface but you will soon realize that space is being created in your life for something new to emerge."

- Eckhart Tolle

"Spirit will conduct a Divine orchestration of people, places, events, circumstances, and synchronicities in radical support of your dreams. You don't have to do it all. You don't have to figure it all out. You are not alone."

- Theresa Rose

"The problems that exist in the world today cannot be solved by the level of thinking that created them."

– Albert Einstein

"Our deepest fear is not that we are inadequate. Our deepest fear is that we are powerful beyond measure. It is our Light, not our Darkness, that most frightens us."

- Marianne Williamson

"The key to the magic kingdom
is to just show up."

- Jyoti

"I so happy!"

- Emma Rose at age 3

Theresa Rose

Acknowledgements

WThank you to my friend and business coach Mark LeBlanc who gently yet firmly pushed me to complete this book, and to my daughter Emma who reminds me every day how BIG a heart can grow when it is full of love.

About the Author

Theresa Rose is a nationally acclaimed business and motivational speaker, award-winning author of four books, entrepreneurial mentor and hardcore hoopdancer who helps individuals and organizations increase engagement and expand into their fullest potential. Prior to launching her speaking career, Theresa was a senior manager of marketing and product development for a Fortune 100 company, a management consultant specializing in process improvement and rapid product implementation, and the owner of a cool, hippy-dippy alternative healing center in Florida.

Theresa was named a top five finalist in the "So You Think You Can Speak?" competition and delivered an electrifying TEDxTalk called "The Hoop Revolution" at TEDxSarasota.

She was honored to serve as the President of the Minnesota Chapter of the National Speakers Association, the premier association for professional speaking. Theresa combines humor, authenticity and her visually stunning hoop performances with rock-solid, actionable content to help organizations cultivate stronger leaders, improve sales and service, and re-engage the zombie workforce.

The stage is Theresa's natural habitat, her daughter Emma is the light in her life (and sometimes her greatest challenge!), and her beloved hula hoop is her favorite teacher. For more information on Theresa, visit TheresaRose.com.

Book Theresa Rose

If you are looking for a speaker that will help your organization Sell More, Lead Stronger and Live Better, Theresa is the speaker for you. Her electrifying presentations deliver the energy, content, value and ROI you need to make a lasting impact.

• Cultivate and leverage the power of emotional value that moves your customers to gladly part with their money.

• Execute Mindful Marketing that focuses on compelling storytelling that leads to increased conversion.

• Create a joy-infused culture that gets your team to want to come to work every day—and actually work.

Theresa taps into her extensive background as an organizational leader, sales and marketing executive, and electrifying performer to deliver customized programs that are perfectly tied to your organizational mission and event theme.

Here are some of the ways Theresa can add value to your next event:

Vegas-style entertainment with captivating stories and infectious comedy

Memorable key takeaways designed to be leveraged long after the event is over

Master of Ceremonies, Panel Facilitation and Breakout Sessions

Invest in Theresa for your conference, sales team event or leadership training today!

Theresa@TheresaRose.com

– 952-456-1670

www.ingramcontent.com/pod-product-compliance
Lightning Source LLC
Chambersburg PA
CBHW072022060426
42449CB00034B/1742